WHAT DO YOU EXPECT?
Discovering methods for deep calm

chad prevost

The Big Self School is a personal growth learning community, whose central mission is to help you deepen your self-knowledge so that you can improve your life. We create digital courses, online community, books, and media designed to activate self-awareness, deeper connections, bold action, and healthy habits so you can play big without burning out.

www.bigselfschool.com

Printed in the United States of America
Text layout and design: Averil Eagle Brannen
Library-of-Congress Control Number is available upon request.
ISBN: 978-1-945064-20-3
eISBN: 978-1-945064-21-0

OTHER BOOKS FROM THE BIG SELF SCHOOL:

- **DESIRE:** How Do You Want To Feel?

- **HOW TO BUILD SELF KNOWLDGE:** Discovering Who You Are

- **WHO DO YOU THINK YOU ARE?** 365 meditations + the books they came from

WHAT DO YOU EXPECT?
Discovering methods for deep calm

FOREWORD

WE HELP PEOPLE TO BE THEMSELVES.

Sounds simple enough, doesn't it? On the one hand, it's true. There is great simplicity and insight into finally realizing that all social reformation and revelation begins with the individual. The harder part is discovering authentic principles and living by them day by day, moment by moment.

One of the most fascinating things about this work is discovering for ourselves that there is no defining characteristic of those who have found themselves. What do we mean "found themselves"? We mean that you were born exactly who you needed to be. You possess gifts and a unique constellation of atoms and neurons all firing to make you already whole. You will find by cutting through outward expectations and cultural mania that within you is already a calm and steady self. Finding yourself begins with finding calm.

Our modern lifestyle packs a punch when it comes to stress. We are bombarded with ideas that we can control the uncontrollable, bend reality to meet our expectations, and twist other people's wills to meet our needs. We have an arsenal of irrational thought patterns that don't jibe with our lived experience, and that dissonance we feel is anxiety showing up. As comedian William Saroyan once quipped, "Everybody has got to die, but I have always believed an exception would be made in my case."

Even in the best of times, our anxiety can dictate the terms of our reality. In times of intensity and heightened stress, our desire to stay calm, patient, and unruffled may seem impossible. Our brains are hard-wired to scan for impending threats in order to keep us safe, and the body automatically keeps score. We can't escape this. We can learn to work with what is naturally happening so that it doesn't pull us under into the deep black waters of anxiety and despair.

ONE

What do we talk about when we talk about calm?

Many mistake calm for passivity. Many others think it is merely about proper breathing diaphragmatically. It is not. Make no mistake, calm is active. Calm is action. Calm is disciplined. The good news is calm can be taught. Breathing techniques can aid calm, but in the final analysis, calm comes from your thoughts.

Calm is one of the most important building blocks of self-knowledge. While there is no one place to begin on the journey to self-knowledge and self-understanding, calm is fundamental.

Calm is related to the concept of *apatheia*. For the Stoics, this meant eradicating the tendency to react emotionally or egotistically to external events, the things that cannot be controlled. It was the optimum rational response to the world. Why? Because of the predictable chaos of the will of others and nature — forces outside ourselves.

Only your own will can be controlled. That does not imply that you lose feeling, or disengage from the world. Ryan Holiday has recently popularized the term apatheia as noted from one early practitioner of the day, Lucius Annaeus Seneca, Rome's greatest playwright, and perhaps also its greatest philosopher. He writes of this concept in *Stillness is the Key*:

> "It's a powerful idea made all the more transcendent by the remarkable fact that nearly every other philosophy of the ancient world — no matter how different or distant — came to the exact same conclusion."

Whether you were a pupil of Confucius in 500 BCE, a student of the early Greek philosopher Democritus one hundred years later, or in Epicurus's garden a generation after that, "You would have heard equally emphatic calls for this imperturbability, unruffledness, and tranquility."

The term is most directly connected to the word stillness in English. It is the ability to be steady as the world storms around. Stillness is the process of achieving deep inner calm. All the great religions and philosophical schools have a term for finding it, and for what it permits. It permits us access into the Tao, the Logos. Stillness, solitude, and silence are all practices that lead to an emotional energy of calm.

Calm and Anger

Seneca called anger the most "savage of all the emotions," and wrote *De Ira (On Anger)* on how you should *never* — under any circumstances — give in to your anger. It may be the most systematic argument against anger ever written. Need justified revenge? Fine. But pursue it for the right reasons, not in anger.

Anger creates haste. Anger blinds. Anger conquers the mind. Anger, according to Seneca's eloquent treatise, is effectively the root of evil. You don't want it in your house. The worst things we do to one another are committed in anger. If anyone would know, it was Seneca, who wrote *De Ira* having survived a first-hand seat in the court of Caligula. The atrocities committed by Caligula, followed shortly after by Nero, cannot be adequately summarized in a sentence; they were nothing less than grotesque and monstrous.

Yet, you might push back and say, "Seneca was an exemplar. He and other Stoics were uncommon humans with great teachers and early fortune. What about the great vast ocean of humanity?"

It's true, and you could say that anger exists within us for a reason. Doesn't anger fuel the athlete to dig deeper? The angry "chip on the shoulder" in any field, for any number of reasons, can drive you for years. Some say they can harness their anger into action, especially for things that are morally wrong. For his part, Seneca says to keep it strictly out in all responses.

In the social sciences over roughly the course of the past century, anger has been viewed as destructive when it is habitual and impulsive. However, anger has also been viewed as *instructive*. "Healthy anger" can be a justified and even necessary response, a sign that you have been wronged, or are experiencing disrespect — whether in fact or perception. Self-respecting people know when their boundaries are being violated.

Anger is also deeply ingrained in our emotions. I'm thinking about all those hundreds of road trips I've made on the U.S. interstates and the growing aggression I feel, especially as the roads congest and the trip's estimated duration lengthens. I think about waiting in long lines at Disney World, like an hour and a half for a three-minute Minions ride while everyone bakes in the heat and gets dehydrated because their $12 Icees are giving them headaches. Or why have Shelley and I had our biggest fights almost every time we travel — the big wonderful event we've been planning for months?

Calm is about staying mindful and in control through a myriad of possible emotions or emotional responses. Anger is but one of them. Angry people are examples of those who are not in control of their minds. Their minds rule them and ultimately keep them in their more primal, animal nature.

In *The 48 Laws of Power*, Robert Greene sums up the anger response — and our response to an angry outburst — superbly:

> "Our anger often stems from problems in our childhood, from the problems of our parents which stem from their own childhood, on and on. Our anger also has roots in the many interactions with others, the accumulated disappointments and heartaches that we have suffered. An individual will often appear as the instigator of our anger but it is much more complicated, goes far beyond what that individual did to us. If a person explodes with anger at you (and it seems out of proportion to what you did), you must remind yourself that it is much larger, goes way back in time, involves dozens of prior hurts, and is actually not worth the bother to understand. Instead of seeing it as a personal grudge, look at the emotional outburst as a disguised power move, an attempt to control or punish you cloaked in the form of hurt feelings and anger."

Why? Because this at least lets you respond with clarity and the appropriate energy. Don't become ensnared in their emotions. Keeping your head while they lose theirs is its own power.

But what about when the anger isn't coming from someone else, but yourself? In psychology, anger is generally considered a primary emotion (along with fear, sadness, and joy). But is it realistic to keep anger "out of our house" altogether? What if we grew up in a family that thwarted our anger response? What if we grew up under conditions that expressed anger openly?

If you feel you have pent up anger within you, this may be a signal that you should confront the source. Repressed anger leads to depression. Frequently expressed anger is also a signal that you are at war with yourself.

In his book *Wishful Thinking*, theologian and novelist Frederich Buechner describes anger like this:

> "Of the Seven Deadly sins, anger is possibly the most fun. To lick your wounds, to smack your lips over grievances long past, to roll over your tongue the prospect of bitter confrontations still to come, to savor to the last toothsome morsel both the pain you are given and the pain you are giving back — in many ways it is a feast fit for a king. The

> chief drawback is that what you are wolfing down is yourself. The skeleton at the feast is you."

If anger is a part of your story, simply learning anger control techniques won't work all that well. What is most effective in working through past anger is to allow it to be confirmed, validated, and released in a safe, controlled environment. Trauma and recovery therapists say you should permit it to be expressed to those who originally sourced it — either by what they did or didn't do.

For many, that may be the only way to make peace. Anger will not let you keep it at a distance for long if the problem goes deep. It needs to be brought forth and given a voice. It should be honored for its felt legitimacy if you are to heal through it and find calm.

Calm and fear

As a general rule, humans are terrible at dealing with uncertainty. Your anxiety wants you to solve problems as quickly as possible. When the world is burning, it's normal to run to the closest fire and stomp it out.

But of course, there's always another fire.

Anxiety creeps upon us. We might start feeling exhausted, overwhelmed, unable to focus. We might get irritated or annoyed at anyone getting too near us at the grocery store during a pandemic when people are supposed to be social distancing, and against our better nature we see everyone as a viral threat. We may not be able to fall asleep at night because our minds remain fully alert and full of things we need to do.

This leads us to focus on the physical symptoms and sensations of anxiety and to overlook the psychological ones. It can lead us to focus on techniques to reduce our anxiety like deep breathing or exercising or meditation or yoga. These practices are great for accessing temporary calm (and will be discussed later in this book), but they still do not get to the root cause of our fear and anxiety.

Cognitive science and rational-emotive therapy have shown us how powerful our beliefs can be. As young children, we have consistent thought patterns based on how we perceived our holding environment, and over time those thought patterns become internalized beliefs. We carry these beliefs into adulthood.

Cognitive flexibility is perhaps one of the greatest tools in the pursuit of accessing calm. There are two components to cognitive flexibility: change how you think about a problem, and let go of what isn't working.

The belief that we can change or control reality can keep us in an anxiety death grip. The root of our stress and anxiety emerges when expectations don't agree with reality. Our mind looks for ways to close the loop. It attempts to ruminate, catastrophize, and play out potential endings. Without the tools — and the courage — to confront the source of our fear, we will be hounded by anxiety.

Some fears don't have a fix. Some fears remind us of our impermanence and stoke existential angst that can feel over-whelming. We fear for our own safety and those of the people we love. Our desire for control doesn't jibe with the truth — we know we are not in control.

Rigid thinking is the opposite of cognitive flexibility. Marcus Aurelius lived through a plague, constant sieges, and betrayals during the last 14 years of his life. But as he wrote in his book *Meditations*, we can always return to that "inner citadel" of peace and imperturbability from which he could much more effectively fight all the challenges he had to face. Fixed mindsets and rigid thinking will keep you looping and looping on the merry-go-round. It may be safe, but the ride is predictable and boring.

We can't know the "work" Aurelius did to get there. Perhaps it was through writing the meditations themselves. After all, tradition tells us that he was writing the meditations as if to himself, not for posterity. We do know that getting to the root can help us to genuinely diminish the anxiety — and better understand ourselves.

Rising above the personal and "normal" response

When my bike was stolen from my outdoor shed, I took it personally. Why me? Why my bike? Didn't the thief realize that to make the money required to buy a new bike would take savings and a lot of hard work, not to mention shopping? How many bike rides would I lose out on, and how would it affect my ability to take my kids on rides?

Why my neighborhood? Why my shed? And this is why we have to lock everything all the time because there are people who don't respect the property of others and believe it is their right as much as anyone's to what they don't have.

When bad things happen, it's easy to take it personally.

On the flip side, when good things happen, it's easy to take that personally too. The truth is, we are better off not taking either personally. That is if we want to practice calm. This goes back to the term apatheia discussed in the opening. Finding stillness involves a process that detaches from the ego's operating instructions as it responds to life vicissitudes.

By contrast, attachment in Buddhist and Hindi practice is seen as the inability to practice or embrace detachment and is seen as the main obstacle towards a serene and fulfilled life. Many spiritual traditions identify the lack of detachment with the continuous worries and restlessness produced by desire and personal ambitions.

In terms of seeking the sources of calm, that is as good a place as any. Don't take the daily humiliations personally. For that matter, don't take the rewards and recognitions either. The rise and fall of your position say nothing about you as a person. Treat both success and failure with indifference. Focus on doing and being your best. If the effort is enough let it be enough. Develop immunity to the seduction of external events. As the last great emperor and Stoic philosopher, Marcus Aurelius who was in power from 161 to 180 AD said, "Receive without pride, let go without attachment."

Don't take life so personally. Take it seriously, but follow it with a dose of levity. Certainly it is virtuous to aspire "to receive without pride," but perhaps it is harder to receive critique especially when it is not what anyone sees or values. Maybe it's even harder when it comes to the smaller things, the things of less prestige and when they irritate us.

Accepting life's "daily humiliations" is what Richard Rohr is talking about in *Falling Upward*, and David Brooks in *The Second Mountain*. It's all a part of growing up and accepting life fluidly as it comes.

Many begin climbing the "second mountain" of life only after life has had a chance to deliver them some failures and setbacks, which may or may not have come out of their own making. Often it comes about in what is roughly drawn up to be the second half of life. The life journey marches on, but now our kids are well on their way out of the house, or our career is revealing itself for what it is (or isn't). Only then do we retreat from the ego's outward-looking stance, and begin the great journey inward.

Although it's not likely, you can begin the journey earlier. Of course, it takes strength and courage to begin the journey at any time of life.

One of the popular methods for finding calm over the past several decades in Western culture has been a practice taken from Buddhism. It is a style of meditation in which we release thoughts through concentrated focus. The aim is to reveal the "monkey mind," the way our thoughts are restless and often aimless and transitory. With discipline and focus this approach begins to inform us about the trivialities of things in our mind that seem big at the moment. It can help us achieve serenity and reduce anxiety. It can give us perspective — a 35,000-foot view — of our ego. Studies have shown that master meditators are less defensive than those who do not meditate, which is also an indication of fluidity and resilience, key tools for sustaining calm.

The emptying of the mind is not the only way to achieve calm. There are ways to analyze and interpret our actions and our thoughts in order to develop the "calm muscle." Active reflection and critical feedback are critical approaches to understanding the chaos we experience in our modern life. Transitory or not, we would do well to accept that anxieties will always be with us. We should make a practice to bring them to consciousness, and actively reflect on where they are coming from, and what our enlightened response should be.

By reflecting and analyzing we can seek to understand. By understanding we can grow. We can seek a variety of sources, and ultimately we can come to expect the unexpected, and laugh at ourselves when we inevitably fail.

What is going on in our brains when we feel irritated with others?

The smaller things, those attached with less prestige, are often the very sources of conflict that we are not prepared for. From a neuropsychological standpoint, it's generally accepted that when people reflexively react to perceived stress in a way that's out of proportion to any direct physical threat, the source is the brain's "primitive" subcortical and limbic region.

The more sophisticated prefrontal cortex isn't slowing the activating event (it may be fatigued from having already done so numerous times over). In response to the anxiety or the continual heightened nervous system arousal, the brain triggers emotional responses, including irritability and even anger.

If another's behavior is seen as annoying, or wrong, we feel a response that tells us that we are not the problem. Someone else is. This can have a temporary calming effect. Our brain is wired to respond this way to manage distress. We blame or focus on others' real or perceived flaws as a way of calming ourselves down.

But that simply explains what is going on when we have "normal" responses. What we aspire to do is to lead the mind, and not let the mind lead us.

TWO

Setting expectations with yourself: Careful what you wish for

If there is one thing you can say about us humans, we are not only creatures of habit, we are creatures of expectations. We amble about with all manner of preconceived ideas about how things are supposed to go — the vast majority of which aren't conscious at all — nor very realistic. The truth is, life is expectation management. The recurring question may very well be: "Well, what do you expect?" It's not just rhetorical. You really do have to keep trying to figure out what to expect from other people and events.

So what can you expect from yourself?

Albert Einstein once remarked, "A man should look for what is, and not for what he thinks should be." Holding high standards of yourself can be a virtue, but only if you're able to manage them in a way that uplifts you and those around you. By contrast, lowering your standards can also be a virtue, especially if it uplifts you and those around you. How do you lift yourself and others up? By maintaining calm in the face of chaos. The practice is often developed when there is no chaos, but practice leads to ever-better development (not perfection), and you should jump in whenever you're ready.

What people call empathy, forgiveness, compassion, sympathy, or charity is often, if not always, a matter of lowering your expectations of other people. Life is easy for no one. Existence itself can be a struggle. The deeper reality to finding calm within compassion is to do so without an inkling of looking down on the person you are serving. Deep joy and understanding come from embracing our shared humanity.

Expectations are shaped in obvious and unconscious ways. We may love breezy, temperate days but based upon years of living where we do, we realize these aren't readily available in the bleak of winter. Based upon those expectations, we aren't tossing chairs across the kitchen when a bitter rain sets in. Similarly, when the car suddenly won't start, we find ourselves upset. Our expectation, and possibly the urgency to get wherever it was we were about to go, has been disrupted.

We expect our waiter to give us service at a restaurant without having to ask for it. We expect the person in front of us to go when the light turns green. We expect the subway to be crowded.

Expectations are performing in our thinking even when we don't realize it. This is just as true for the expectations we have for ourselves and for others. Expectations guide our responses.

Expectations can also give us a sense of motivation and direction, or help us meet certain standards. But how do we start to manage personal expectations (or the real or perceived expectations of others) instead of letting them rule our lives?

We tend to expect a lot of ourselves. Unfortunately, our expectations are often unrealistic, which can cause a lot of stress and self-criticism, so it's important to manage them well. We want stuff when we want it, and that can make us hard on ourselves.

Ambition is necessary for innovation and can be a part of your authentic inner drive and purpose, but if you expect to instantly achieve your goals, it's a guaranteed recipe for anxiety and frustration. Be mindful of your own timeline as you set goals and objectives, and make sure you have a realistic plan. When things go wrong, or situations change, work on developing emotional awareness. Bringing emotions into active consciousness can help you pause, and give that prefrontal cortex a little more time to respond. You're not always going to respond like Marcus Aurelius, but you can get better at responding in a thinking framework and not an emotional one.

It's easy to feel like a failure when things shift, or goals prove harder than they at first seemed to be to achieve. We sometimes try to blindly continue without reconsidering our expectations. Instead, pause and consider your options, reframe that initial expectation in the context of your new situation. Why is it really so important? What would an adjustment mean?

When our lives are ruled by personal expectations, it can make every day a struggle. Think of yourself as an explorer going through life, rather than someone with a path dictated by expectations. Whether you succeed or fail, a more realistic and resilient expectation should simply be to learn as you go.

Author, Kamal Ravikant, went to a Buddhist monastery for a silent retreat. After he finished, the teacher said the monks were available to speak with anyone who wanted to. Ravikant thought for a while, then went up to one of the monks and asked, "How do you find peace?"

The monk laughed and said, "Oh, an easy one, huh?"

Ravikant laughed too but then was surprised by the monk's followup.

"I say yes. To everything that happens, I say yes."

Ravikant shares his interpretation of the monk's advice: "Most of our pain, most of our suffering, comes from resistance to what is. Life is. And when we resist what life is, we suffer. When you can say yes to life, surrender to life and say: 'Okay, what should I be now?' That's where power comes from."

We would add that it's not merely power, but the power to remain fluid, to remain in a state of acceptance or apatheia, that is a true path to deep calm.

Process over perfection

We sometimes may find ourselves using the phrase, "Rome wasn't built in a day" to remind ourselves that something great took a very long time to develop. In fact, if you unpack it, it's a striking metaphor. According to what we know of the history, it took almost exactly nine centuries for Rome to evolve from original settlements of clay huts to the urban metropolis it became until the time of Marcus Aurelius.

The evolution was anything but a perfect graphic curve of growth. The city was sacked and burned at one point. It went through cycles of expansion and it contracted into a defensive position from sieges on a variety of fronts. There were civil wars, horrific leaders. All of the drama and spectacle notwithstanding, there was nevertheless an overarching trend of development. Within a lifespan it was probably hard — if not impossible — to trace.

Similarly, within our own lives, even when we've embraced a specific goal, even when the goal is full of challenge and reward, and maybe even when it is high on our list of what we would describe as fulfilling, it may be hard to track our development on a daily basis. Even for those of us obsessed with measurements and spreadsheet tracking and analysis, we could easily get frustrated by the small measure of progress that is made even through strong effort.

I ran for the cross-country team in high school, and I was pretty good, lettering my freshman year. I kept up with running sporadically throughout my 20s, finding it a mental and emotional release. Usually, the activity of the running wasn't exactly easy, but the way you felt after even just a two or three-mile run was fantastic.

I took it up again in my early 30s. My first race after around six weeks of running was 4.7 miles, and I averaged an 8:45 mile. That felt very slow. My expectation was that I would perform much better than that, and it may have been fueled by my competitive pride. My friend had run a 7:30 average mile. He was a little younger than me, but he didn't seem to be training all that much. I knew I could do better.

So I signed up for a 10k (6.4 mile) race with six weeks to prepare. I followed a program. I ate right, remained consistent and disciplined, and upped my mileage every week. I expected to have a major breakthrough now that I was much further along in getting "back into" running. I ran the race at an average speed of 8:30 a mile. Frustrated by how much effort I had put into training for such a small return on improvement, I gradually faded away from running for a long time.

In retrospect, of course, one can say that training over a six-week period isn't enough time to expect dramatic improvement in results. So an expectation adjustment would be in order. Also, what really stands out now is: Who cares what your time was? It's about the process, and possibly, the community.

Or what about trying to improve on an instrument, learning a language, or a complex piece of software? We can become discouraged by the enormity of the project in front of us. The frustration that we're not doing enough, not smart enough, not patient enough, simply not enough can easily take hold. If we adjust our expectations, even slightly, not in a pessimistic way, but in a more calm and realistic way, we may very well keep ourselves on the path. The fable of the hare and the tortoise hits the expectation ideal right on the nose. The tortoise grinds at his slow but realistic and sustainable pace and wins.

We may think of our billable hours as "special hours" because we are so efficient and productive with our time. We may see the bathroom upgrades as a weekend construction project because we think we know exactly what it takes to put in the 4-8 hours of work to take out the tub and re-tile the floor. We think we'll write that next great novel in 90 days because we know we're capable of writing at least 1,000 words a day.

On the one hand, you could say that giving yourself impossibly high goals, or at least challenging ones, helps you strive to reach as high a mark as possible, always striving "to do your best." But if your value really is "doing your best," it is probably not realistically going to be executed on a tight deadline. Also, the idea that "anything worth doing is worth doing your best" leads to the tyranny of perfectionism. Sometimes, as per the wisdom of the great child psychologist and moral philosopher D.W. Winnicott, many things — especially daunting things or ongoing tasks — should be done "good enough."

"No, I am at least above average," you say. You're not going down without a fight.

"I will hold myself to above-average standards. I will do more, and I will do it in record time."

Just know you are laying the bed in the garden of anxiety.

Expectations with others:
It's hard to collaborate

As it turns out, setting clear expectations with others is a useful approach to stopping problems before they start, or stopping them in their tracks. Collaboration always sounds easier than it is. While the vast majority would like to think of themselves as collaborators, and even say they "enjoy" collaboration, we are also blind to a lot about ourselves. We can expect others to be blind about themselves.

Collaboration involves a huge variety of interpersonal factors, too many to illustrate here other than to say the foibles, past experiences, as well as the self-expectations of others factor into the equation. Reality proves that successful collaborations are actually quite rare.

Think how hard it is to keep a music band of just three or four members together. Half the battle is staying together and committed even with a whole lot of shared values and backgrounds. A tech startup? They're stress incubators. Can you even name one that isn't (or wasn't)?

Even with your personal expectations well in hand, it can be difficult to change what others expect of you. Invest some time and energy, however, and you can improve your relationships with others. No one knows how to make you happy if they don't know what makes you happy.

So, begin by asking what others expect of you. Then state them to the person or people you're working with. This adds mutual respect and a clear sense of purpose toward shared goals. Or, if there is disagreement about the goals or tension about the expectations, those can be discussed upfront, ahead of the moments when stress is involved and perhaps a deadline is going to be missed, or it becomes clear a goal is not being acted on.

Emotional responses are almost inevitable under stress. Weekly expectation check-ins and adjustments may be necessary to keep unnecessary stress away. Sometimes it may take one good conversation.

Setting expectations with others at work

Timing is everything. If you fix a problem when it's small, you can often make minor adjustments to address it. It's when you don't hear about the issue — the delay, the bug, or the unforeseen problem — that stress snowballs and becomes more difficult to deal with and discuss. It's the difference between a small tweak being sufficient and having to call on all hands to fix it.

No matter what kind of work your team does, there will be unforeseen issues. The monster always rears its head. Maybe something about the way the code was built in the early phases when the company had to outsource the help has led to problems about how to build on top of it. Now, an entire reframing needs to happen. Or the marketing team isn't going to make the deadline for delivering the new graphics package and executing on the product launch's advertising campaign. A hard choice will have to be made. Things should have been thought through more clearly from the beginning. The CEO is looking for someone to blame.

Whatever happens, the ideal way to inculcate a culture of calm is to encourage communication. No one should have to fear delivering the news. Don't kill the messenger if you're in charge, and don't live in fear of being the messenger if you're not.

In the hypercompetitive world of capitalism, you may have a lot of meetings, but in the end actions are what matter. Work is a place where communication happens toward an end goal. Communication is great, but the priorities of the team aren't just to play therapist and constantly discern the blind spots and communication styles of each individual.

There is new data that tells us we like working toward common goals, but the reality is that we don't often actually do the work together. The paradox of working on teams is that they can be both the greatest source of connection and belonging in the workplace, and yet teamwork is some of the loneliest work we ever do. We rarely do the actual work in the presence of the other members on the team. They are busy doing the things *they* are good at.

Interestingly enough, for managers and leaders, for the very reason so much of our work is done alone, you might consider the power of a single word: together. Researchers have found that using this single word with some well-placed repetition gets employees to work nearly 50% longer, stick with problems longer, and focus better. It's almost as if the intrinsic motivation felt by working together gives employees a resilient, flexible mindset. They feel a greater sense of purpose and renewed energy.

So we need a way to experience the psychological-connect-edness of working as a team, even when we technically aren't. As social researcher Heidi Grant writes: "The word 'together' is a powerful social cue to the brain. In and of itself, it seems to serve as a kind of relatedness reward, signaling that you belong, that you are connected, and that there are people you can trust working with you toward the same goal."

As people continue to migrate out to "remote" locations to work with only the occasional bobbing head on our video feeds to check in on how we're doing, we need to recognize our need for connection as it relates to finding calm.

Setting expectations with others in your personal life

Expectations of others are entirely different in scope between the professional and the personal. Expectations can be the enemies of love.

Why is it that no one can disappoint us as much as the people we're in relationship with? It's because of the very expectations we put in these "others." It's because we love them that we've placed our trust in them to one extent or another. And it's because of trust that we place expectations on them.
There is also a direct correlation between the intensity of our love and the level of hopeful expectation. So, when expectations aren't met, we tend to have a heightened level of emotion, and hurtful things are said.

And for all of our "loving" expectations, how often have our loved ones actually lived up to our standards? Hopefully, some have or do meet our high expectations, or at least they do some of the time. If you really think about it, though, it's likely that most of our relationships with others are flawed — or at least we will see them as such — and it is based first and foremost on our expectations.

A recent study from the *Journal of Social and Personal Rela-*

tionships looked at 296 young adults and found that relationship expectation was a predictor of relationship satisfaction — a relationship not matching expectations was a sign of low satisfaction.

Managing and setting expectations can sometimes feel like driving along a ridge road on a foggy night. You can drive off one side expecting people to be able to handle what they can't. You can drive off the other with your own mistakes in personal expectations — and in either case, you can ask too much or too little. Setting expectations and developing the skill to know when they're impacting your reality takes focused steering if we are to keep driving steadily and with as much calm as possible.

Stay positive but realistic.

THREE

Taking charge of the mind and finding focus

"Why do only a few possess a calm mind?" a disciple asked his teacher. The teacher responded with a story about the elephant and the fly.

"An elephant was once picking leaves from a tree," said the teacher. "A small fly came buzzing near his ear. The elephant waved it away with his long ears. The fly came again, and the elephant waved it away once more. After this went on several more times the elephant asked the fly: 'Why are you so restless and noisy? Why can't you stay for a while in one place?'
"The fly answered: 'I am attracted to whatever I see, hear or smell. My five senses, and everything that happens around me, pull me constantly in all directions and I cannot resist them. What is your secret? How can you stay so calm and still?'

"The elephant stopped eating and said: 'My five senses do not rule my attention. I am in control of my attention, and I can direct it wherever I want. This helps me to get immersed in whatever I do, and therefore my mind is focused and calm. Now that I am eating, I am completely immersed in eating.'"

The disciple's eyes widened. He looked at his teacher and

said, "I understand! If I am in command of my five senses, I can disregard sense impressions, and my mind will be calm."

"The mind is restless," said the teacher, "and goes wherever the attention is. Control your attention, and you control your mind."

This is a theme that echoes repeatedly throughout the sayings of the desert Christians. To attend to the poor is to contemplate the mystery of God's presence in the world. Paying attention (both to God and to each other) is fundamental to a meaningful existence, and meaning-making is one of the great sources of calm.

There is a common fable about an "Egyptian father" seeking a sign of divine approval for his long years of monastic devotion. He is told that his sanctity is nothing compared to a common grocer in a nearby town. The monk found the grocer occupied with his vegetables amid the noise and hurry of the city streets, attentive to the needs of all those coming to him. Even as night came on, with the people growing rowdy, singing loudly in the streets, the man stayed at his task, helping latecomers with their needs.

In exasperation the monk blurted out, "How can you pray with noise like this?"

The grocer looked around and answered very simply. "I tell myself they're all going to the kingdom," he said. "They're concentrating with single-minded attention on what they do, singing songs with all the joy they can muster. See how they prepare for the kingdom of God without even knowing it! How can I do less than to praise in silence the God they inadvertently celebrate in song?"

That night the old monk walked slowly back to his cell, realizing he had received — from a common grocer — an important lesson in the craft of attentiveness.

It is as if granting each other the gift of your attention frees you to find your focus, and find your calm. It's not that one necessarily only needs to focus on others. It is also, as with the elephant and the fly, to take control of your mind — and therefore tap into the source of calm — through increasing your focus and attention on any task.

The challenge of course is that with so many possible tasks, what to choose? What kind of task is worthy of your focused attention?

The craftsman's spirit

There are many ways to find focus, and through it to find calm and satisfaction. Before we look at a few approaches — both within and outside of ourselves — let's first consider the concept of *shokunin kishitsu*.

It is roughly translated as "the craftsman's spirit." In Europe the concept of putting your full love and attention into your craft tends to come from chefs and higher levels of sophistication. The core concept is Japanese, and it is meant for all endeavors. It is the concept of giving your full attention to whatever the task is at hand, however seemingly small and commonplace. For instance, at first glance the Tokyo airport may seem dull and ordinary, but as you look around you notice how clean and neat it is, the deeply polished floors. A knife handle may be made with simplicity, but that does not mean it is poorly crafted. The elegant simplicity is saying, in effect, "Use me as you choose, in whatever way suits your skills."

The concept applies to any task. It can imbue our consciousness with gratitude and focus. It can slow us down.

Patience leads to slow growth, which leads to calm

Hurry creates haste. Haste never realizes that careful foundation work is the quickest in the end. Hurry is the scourge of Western civilization, especially in the United States, but well beyond and into almost any urban population connected to the great global economic machinery. It is both a cause and a result of our high-pressure civilization.

Men, in their desire to provide for the future happiness of their family, often sacrifice the present happiness for the allure of more and faster. Men forget their place in the home is more than merely "breadwinning." Through the nonstop pressure to "grind" and "crush it" they leave the home for countless hours every day, leaving the less prestigious work of domesticity to women. It's an age-old story that has its roots so deeply dug into the narrative of our culture and family life that a few waves of feminism have only begun to disrupt.

It's not just men that are in great haste. Women and men are rushing faster and faster to check the boxes on their calendars and provide to the needs of endless expectations. It's a cultural legacy we hand down from generation to generation.

We see courageous and successful entrepreneurs on our

screens. They're inescapable if we're on our various media channels. They purport to be harbingers of what we too can become if only we grind a little harder, make sacrifices with a little more discipline, and follow the "secrets" or the "keys" or the right step-by-step template.

We take a few steps, but something breaks down. We find we can't get to sleep on time because of roommates or children or our own anxieties, and we struggle to get up early enough. Or we put ourselves "out there" and are met with hostility, or more often, indifference. We aren't getting the likes and the downloads we need. We become anxious. We doubt. We lose our calm and decide this isn't for us. It must be the better people who have made it to the top.

In fact, as so many "at the top" will tell you, there's a terrific amount of luck involved. Sometimes those who have made it to great fortune and/or fame actually haven't worked as hard as a great many who aren't famous or financially in the top 1%. These are the rules, not the exceptions.

The exceptions we hear about. Their algorithms are trending at the top of the platforms. They possess the thing we want. They say we can do it in 21 days, or 21 weeks, or whatever the number and whatever the secret, they promise if we do it right we can achieve it fast.

Meanwhile, life is passing us by. Our kids are passing through the grades like sands in the hourglass. Our "windows of opportunity" are shrinking. We want to be drinking margaritas and watching the sunset out our beach window. We want to wear sandals and take long walks on the beach and have time just to chat with our friends and neighbors with no particular place to go.

But in order to get there, wherever the fantasy is, however grounded in possibility or wildly imagined, we first have lots to do, and we have to do them each and every day and then each and every week and month. We have to crank. We have to dig. No pain, no gain. Just do it. The inspirational mottos and cheerleading messages are endless. Then you wake up ten years later and wonder where you've even gotten for all the frantic pace.

We hear from the people staring you down through the camera when what we could really use would be hearing the struggle of the vast majority who are nowhere to be seen. How many different role models could we learn from who could show us the far more familiar patterns? How many times have we spent years on a career path only to realize in spite of our striving it wasn't the direction we intended, that our ladder, as Thomas Merton put it, "was leaning on the wrong wall?" How many mistaken assumptions, how many wrong turns, how many times have you enthusiastically jumped into ideas that led nowhere?

And the fact is, time is limited. Some of us find limitless creative ways to deny death's looming presence. Many of us, by contrast, are only too aware. We feel we have so much in us, so much possibility, so many things we want to see, things we want to do.

Like many other virtuous actions, finding calm takes courage. It takes courage to disrupt your current state of operations. It takes courage to admit you've wasted some time, maybe a lot of time. It takes courage to accept that not everything you're going to want to do, or that you are able to do, will get accomplished. It takes courage to recognize these limitations because it invites sadness. There may even be a necessary grieving depending on the extent and intensity of the dreams.

When you can come to an acceptance of the limitation of time you have, you are more likely to find calm at the end of the tunnel. "The spirit is willing, but the flesh is weak," as the apostle Paul put it. Inevitably, tragic as it is for the way we have evolved as a species, our desires and imaginations will always outperform the actual potential we have to bring them into realization.

You can choose to live a harried, frustrated, anxious life checking off boxes just to prove the last paragraph wrong, to demonstrate how you are in fact the exception. Or you can accept unfulfilled desires as a part of life.

One thing is important to remember as you journey toward calm: don't be anxious about finding calm. Say "yes" to experience as it comes. "Let the game come to you," coaches tell athletes. Play within yourself. Slow down. Calm doesn't have to be hard. What is hard? Maintaining all the illusions. Always rushing.

Finding calm outside yourself

IN NATURE

It's strangely calming to be absorbed in the contemplation of something vastly bigger than ourselves. Belden C. Lane explores the concept between spirituality and geography in-depth in The Solace of Fierce Landscapes. His thesis is that geography shapes our vision of the transcendent, and in especially "fierce" or dramatic and unforgiving landscapes — like deserts and high mountains and remote places "far from the madding crowd" — we are even more drawn to God or what you could call the Transcendent.

It's not only dramatic landscapes that transport us. It can be something as simple as a sunset. We tend to associate sunsets with coasts because we are perhaps more aware of the open sky on a coast. Often when we're in a coastal community we're there to relax in the first place, and we pay attention to the sun's multicolored splendor as it descends into oblivion.

But what about the time you see a sunset at an unexpected moment? Like when I drop my eighth-grader off at school. We're talking about his daily grind, maybe a reminder to keep consistent with his homework, or how to deal with a teacher that doesn't seem to like him, and as we top the hill, there it is in the open sky — the sunrise (in this case). It's like looking at something bigger than yourself and being momentarily comforted by the fact.

Or you're driving in dense traffic to the airport with a cacophony of work voices in your head. You're frustrated with the traffic, and you're frustrated that the contract probably isn't going to be signed without some serious renegotiation. You're forming your responses ahead of time in your mind because you know the CEO is going to be pissed. Then, boom: a beautiful sunset opens up along the skyline. If you didn't have to keep your eyes on the road, everything seems smaller and, somehow, this eases your mind.

On the Sublime, attributed to the 3rd-century Greek rhetorician Cassius Longinus, ascribed the purpose of poetry to be of "a lofty, ennobling seriousness." The concept took hold in the 18th century among English philosophers, critics, and poets who associated the sublime with "overwhelming sensation." In *A Philosophical Inquiry into the Origin of our Ideas of the Sublime and the Beautiful*, Edmund Burke identified the sublime as the experience of the infinite, which is both terrifying and thrilling because it threatens to overpower the importance of human enterprise in the universe.

By contrast, the rationalist school of thought asserts that knowledge of innate ideas can be arrived at through intuition and reasoning alone. Burke argued that the passions, as revealed through our imagination, truly shapes how and what we see, hear, and feel in the world.

The sublime, then, is our strongest passion, and it is grounded in terror. As Rainer Maria Rilke writes in the very first line of *The Duino Elegies*, "Every angel is terrifying." Yet the terror is not exclusively an unpleasant emotion, for danger or pain can, in certain circumstances, give us delight. And the sublime has other qualities: it overwhelms our faculty of reason.

The Romantic ideal attempts to swing the pendulum back from being in the head to being in the "heart" (for lack of a better word), and that way is achieved through the calm found in nature. Just considering the timelessness and emptiness of a desert is enough to put things in perspective. Year by year little will change. Take a simple path in the woods. The same rock you step over at age five will be the same rock you step over at 85.

Whether comparing ourselves to others or caught up in the minutiae of details we have to tend to, we find ourselves in distress. Sometimes we push harder to "prove our value" as we say. Sometimes we give ourselves pep talks, or by contrast, the inner critic comes out and we self-loathe. We'd be more successful if only it weren't for _____. Then you'll learn some small fact about new evidence of how rivers ran on Mars for hundreds of thousands of years about 3.5 billion years ago. Or you'll gaze first hand down at the little valley below. Next to the mountain or the relative timelessness of a distant planet (and the prospect of a teaming life there much like our own now), and then the CEO's disappointment, or the person whose faster or smarter or richer than you, doesn't seem like such a big deal.

As Wendell Berry puts it in "The Peace of Wild Things":

> When despair for the world grows in me
> And I wake in the night at the least sound
> In fear of what my life and my children's lives may be,
> I go and lie down where the wood drake
> Rests in his beauty on the water, and the great heron feeds.
> I come into the peace of wild things…"

And "for a time" he (the speaker of the poem) rests in the "grace of the world" and finds freedom.

Nature transports us out of ourselves and gives us perspective. The concerns of all humankind become small in comparison, much less those of a single person. Nature calms us not merely because it is sometimes "tranquil," but because it is indifferent to us, and because of its sheer scope and scale.

IN TRAVEL

Speaking of being transported, many find calm by finally breaking through the confines of conventional and ordinary living and choosing to travel. The late 20th-century philosopher Alan Watts once used this analogy in a lecture: "If I draw a circle, most people, when asked what I have drawn, will say I've drawn a circle or a disc, or a ball. Very few people will say I've drawn a hole in the wall, because most people think of the inside first, rather than thinking of the outside. But actually these two sides go together — you cannot have what is 'in here' unless you have what is 'out there.'"

You might cringe at the idea of travel as being a process of calm. Going to the airport hours in advance, getting practically mugged going through security and flying in the tightly confined space of a plane. Or it could be the slog of many long tedious hours in a car or on a bus. But the act of being in a foreign environment and meeting new people surprisingly help many become more confident. That confidence allows you to overcome fears and fight anxiety.

When you travel you also have to live much more in the moment. You notice things around you, you have better conversations, you focus on your appreciation of the world. There is also freedom in not constantly being tethered to devices and (therefore) media. When you're not looking down at your phone or computer screen you find yourself using all your senses to take in the world.

Travel challenges you to pay attention to people, places, and ideas that we tend to brush over in our day-to-day. Where we are is critical to understanding who we are. And we are in many places at once within the contexts of our lives. While many wonder what travelers are "seeking to find," the truth is that the seeking is the finding for many. Traveling, too, leads to many of the revelations discussed about nature. It transports your self-understanding.

IN MUSIC

Baroque music, especially the slower movements, the largos, adagios, and andantes, have been proven to slow the mind. In fact, they were intentionally created to do just that. Commissioned as it was from the church, you could almost call the Baroque period (generally from about 1600 until Bach's death in 1750) a grand experiment in creating music that calms the mind.

Baroque's slower tempos have roughly the same number of beats per minute as the human heart. The music has also been shown in various studies to shift the brain from its normal beta rhythms to alpha rhythms. The alpha rhythms are the most conducive to creativity and learning.

Of course from long before that in a broad range of cultures, music has been created as a bridge to other consciousness, often to calm and focus the mind. We tend to think of instruments involving harp, flute, guitar, sitar, or piano. Musical meditation expressions through Hindi religious practices, especially in India have developed highly sophisticated practices. Ragas have become a source of many studies into their efficacy in impacting a listener's emotion, regardless of cultural background.

At the precipice of a third decade into the 21st century, one can now stream limitless approaches to meditation music and the sounds of nature. In general, these characteristics tend to be what is associated with creating the conditions of calm from a scientific brainwave analysis: tempo, rhythmic regularity, and tonality.

IN CHALLENGES, EXERCISE, AND RELAXATION TECHNIQUES

Many find calm through focused attention on expressive creative activity: building birdhouses, creating a music collection, drawing, and painting. Others can find the focus and fulfillment through an earnest challenge, even if it's not "creative" per se. The development of a new skill at something like woodworking or beer brewing or learning a language or instrument can bring calm. Some find calm in challenges like reading or meditating with personal goals.

Exercise is a direct source to calm. The physical benefits of exercise have long been established. Studies show that exercise is effective at reducing fatigue, improving alertness and concentration, and enhancing cognitive function.

Exercise elevates depressed moods. There is evidence to show that active people have lower rates of anxiety and depression than those who are generally sedentary. Exercise helps the brain cope better with stress. According to the Anxiety and Depression Association of America, "In one study, researchers found that those who got regular vigorous exercise were 25 percent less likely to develop depression or an anxiety disorder over the next five years."

Many successful and responsible people feel anxious if they are not always at work, doing something "productive." Even at home, they feel they must always be cleaning, working in the yard, repairing things. There is virtue in work, and it is better than aimless pitter-pattering. But constant busyness is not a recipe for discovering the benefits of calm. As a general rule, alternate between activity and reflection.

To that end, methods of meditation, yoga, and focused journaling are all potent sources for finding and sustaining calm.

There are scores of breathing methods and techniques. Each approach will require different skill sets which, with practice, can become automatic. Cold-water therapy, discussed in the following section, has entire courses focused on breathing techniques that get increasingly challenging and advanced.

The stress response from cold water therapy builds calm

Cold water has been used therapeutically for centuries and has come back into popularity using many different therapies and research programs, in no small part to Wim Hof and a famous practitioner of his methods, Tony Robbins. Hippocrates, "the father of medicine," used cold water in his treatment of the most serious illnesses.

The latest form of cold therapy is cryotherapy and consists of exposure to extremely cold air that is maintained at -110° to -140°C (roughly -166° to -220°F) in cryochambers, generally for 2-3 minutes. It has become popularized among athletes for its possible beneficial effect on recovery and performance.

The Netherlands has seen an increasing trend for cold bathing over the past few years. Part of this growing popularity is owed to the scientific approach of a health and mindset technique developed by Wim Hof. Methods involving concentration, breathing, and cold-exposure have shown to modulate the immune response.

The Wim Hof approach, backed up with compelling research, makes numerous claims:

REDUCED STRESS.

Regularly taking cold showers imposes a small amount of stress on your body, which leads to a process called hardening. This means that your nervous system gradually gets used to handling moderate levels of stress.

HIGHER ALERTNESS.

Cold showers wake your body up, inducing a higher state of alertness. The cold also stimulates you to take deeper breaths, decreasing the level of CO_2 throughout the body, helping you concentrate.

MORE ROBUST IMMUNE RESPONSE.

Cold showers increase the number of white blood cells in your body. These blood cells protect your body against diseases. Researchers believe this process is related to an increased metabolic rate.

INCREASED WILLPOWER.

It takes a strong mind to endure the cold for extended periods of time. By incorporating cold showers into your daily routine, you are strengthening your willpower.

WEIGHT LOSS.

Research has shown that cold showers (and exposure to cold in general), in addition to increasing metabolic rate directly, stimulate the generation of brown fat. Brown fat is a specific type of fat tissue that in turn generates energy by burning calories.

Perspective

If you think about it, whether we're traveling, exercising, meditating, or reveling at the overwhelming majesty of nature, it's all about creating the conditions for a perspective shift. And what is a shift in perspective, but a shift in expectations? Finding calm is about discovering — in the final analysis — that your endeavors are not the big deal you ascribe to them, not really. It's about discovering these things outside of yourself that lead you to a calmer perspective inside yourself.

One of the major perspective shifts we find ourselves needing to unwind is the self-worth we ascribe to what we do. Calm helps us "be." How we choose to be — especially when we're not always doing — is the essential question. Many say that ultimate happiness comes from relationships — from those others outside our "self." We can reflect on the extent to which we may think that is true, especially when even our most valued relationships are often so fraught with challenge and difficulty. They certainly tell us about who we are. How we interact with others is a direct reflection of what is going on within us. Think about that for a minute.

And if what you've got going on is a greater degree of calm than otherwise, then you are going to reciprocate calm in your relationships.

Let us consider the words of William George Jordan from his 1900 book, *The Majesty of Calmness*:

> "A fad lives for a few weeks or months, a philosophy lives through generations and centuries. Accept slow growth if it must be slow, and know the results must come, as you would accept the long, lonely hours of the night,—with absolute assurance that the heavy-leaded moments must bring the morning. Do so, and you will find more calm.
>
> Also, banish the word hurry from your life. Let us care for nothing so much that we would pay honor and self-respect as the price of hurrying it. Let us cultivate calmness, restful-ness, poise, sweetness,—doing our best, bearing all things as bravely as we can; living our life undisturbed by the prosperity of the wicked or the malice of the envious. Let us not be impatient, chafing at delay, fretting over failure, wearying over results, and weakening under opposition. Let us ever turn our face toward the future with confidence and trust, with the calmness of a life in harmony with itself, true to its ideals, and slowly and constantly progressing toward their realization."

Having a calm mind means having an ordered mind. It means being able to sleep deeply. It means thinking with clarity. It doesn't mean "Calm down!" as we were admonished as school kids. It doesn't mean losing your joy or enthusiasm. If anything, its goals are the opposite: fine-tuning your appreciation for what is all around you; seeking balance where life is distorted and chaotic; creating a more joyous, fulfilled, and less anxious way of being.

It is toward the end of finding calm from the ordinary moments of domestic life to the high aims and dreams of our life's purpose that this book is written. May it prove a helpful guide in building frameworks for calm in all your relationships and pursuits.

AFTERWORD

Why do we measure our self-worth against how productive we are?

In fact, even as you engage with the material in this text and are confronted by your personal expectations, and the expectations of others, don't expect dramatic results. That may sound like a counterintuitive claim to make, but it's true. This small book is practicing what it preaches: adjust your expectations.

You don't need this book to tell you that you get out of something what you put into it. You already know that. You aren't looking for glib answers. You're looking for the source, the cause of what is working against your calm.

Thus, if you come to recognize that anxiety, fear, irritation, and even anger will never be fully eliminated, then you're likely to do better finding calm. By contrast, if you begin to feel burdened by trying to achieve calm — and remonstrate yourself every time you regress — you're already setting yourself up for failure. Accept that there will be chaos and that you will not always be able to maintain an idyllic version of stoic calm. Accept that there will be anxiety. It is a permanent feature of life.

While there are certainly joys in travel, there is no Utopia. Actually, in its truest definition Utopia does exist: as an *imagined* place where everything is perfect. Thus, it is also nowhere — except for in our imaginations. And of course, wherever you go, there you are, as Confucious is attributed as having first said. You take your "you" with you to the remote island paradise with the perfect breeze blowing through the windows and the blue water all around you.

You take your "you" with you on your journey for greater status and prestige. You can get the novel published and make the *New York Times* bestseller list, and still you wake up to yourself.

You can be a beautiful and famous person, able to sleep with anyone of your choosing at almost any time of your choosing, but still you wake up to yourself.

You can finally crack the capitalistic code and become one of the .1% and make tens of millions of dollars or more. Still, there is anxiety poking its head around the corner.

On the one hand, this realization alone may be fodder for deeper self-understanding. Why are you driving for one particular aim, goal, or life dream or another? Consider your motives. You may be closer to the calm you truly desire than you know without all the striving. No doubt, there are lots of reasons to be occupied, to be busy, to focus and drive toward goals. It's the motivation behind the occupation that needs to be considered — if calm is what you aspire to.

But beyond that, the main idea is acceptance. Gain a sense of humor about yourself and our collective contradictions and struggles. We become adults, but we regress into childhood patterns all the time. In fact, one thing you'll find as you grow into yourself and discover more sources of calm are all the times you lose control. It may even be that the very type of person who is attracted to the idea of learning more about calm is the person riddled by anxiety. The longing for calm can manifest for the very reason you are not calm.
In the end, it takes courage.

Calm is not anxious to draw conclusions on everything. Calm also prepares one to keep on course even during inevitable hardship, setbacks, and failure.

You can't control the future, but you can begin to work on the version of yourself that you carry into that future. This preparation can feel like slow work, but remember that Rome wasn't built in a day. Also realize that the slow-built things are almost always better than the things made fast. Think of the way a prefab suburban house gets thrown up in days with its cheap materials, then think about the centuries it took to build majestic cathedrals. A mushroom can grow overnight, but it takes decades for the oak to achieve its full height — and it keeps adding growth rings every year.

Recognize how your anxious fixing gets in the way of flexible thinking and creative solutions. Your efforts to manage your anxiety and do your best thinking are investments in yourself and they will pay dividends all the rest of the days of your life. Everything has a shelf-life: your fame, your money, your book, the food in your pantry, the struggles of your children, the struggle at work.

Be still on a regular basis. The work you put in now for your future self lives on.

THE BIG SELF SCHOOL

The Big Self School is a personal growth learning community, whose central mission is to help you deepen your self-knowledge so that you can improve your life. We create digital courses, online community, books, and media designed to activate self-awareness, deeper connections, bold action, and healthy habits so you can play big without burning out.

www.bigselfschool.com

ABOUT THE AUTHOR

Chad Prevost has advanced degrees in creative writing, literature, and theology. A workshop leader and entrepreneur, he has started and participated in writing and literary arts communities in Atlanta, Austin, Chattanooga, and New York. He also has experience writing as a journalist for startups in tech and logistics. He is the author of several books of poetry, as well as interactive-fiction for young adults. He has innovated writing processes to foster reflection and insight, narrative strength, and authentic voice since 2004. Chad supports the Oxford Comma.

www.ingramcontent.com/pod-product-compliance
Lightning Source LLC
Chambersburg PA
CBHW031538260326
41914CB00002B/186